A New True Book

THE SHOSHONI

By Dennis B. Fradin

Consultant:
Bonnie Teton, Coordinator
Shoshoni/Bannock Museum
Fort Hall, Idaho

CHILDRENS PRESS ®

CHICAGO

22 (right), 24
—29
rvice—36
Courtesy Field Museum/© R. Flanagan—12
Thomas Gilcrease Institute of American Art—8, 39
Museum of the American Indian—13 (top left), 37
North American Indian Heritage Center—14, 15, 16 (left), 38
© Chris Roberts—35 (left)
© John Running—Cover, 2, 4 (top left and right), 11, 13 (top right and bottom), 16 (right), 18 (right), 22 (left), 26 (2 photos), 35 (right), 41 (left), 44 (bottom left)
© L. Sheppard/Sho-Ban News—18 (right), 41 (right), 44 (top)
Smithsonian Institution—33, 38
Walters Art Gallery—6, 21, 25
Wyoming Travel Commission—44 (bottom right)
Montana Historical Society—31

Young dancer holding eagle feathers

Library of Congress Cataloging-in-Publication Data

Fradin, Dennis B.
    The Shoshoni / by Dennis B. Fradin.
        p.   cm. — (A new true book)
    Includes index.
    Summary: Describes the history, beliefs, customs, homes, and day-to-day life of the Shoshoni Indians. Also discusses how they live today.
    ISBN 0-516-01156-1
    1. Shoshoni Indians—Juvenile literature. 2. Indians of North America—Northwest, Pacific—Juvenile literature. [1. Shoshoni Indians. 2. Indians of North America—Northwest, Pacific.] I. Title.
E99.S4F73   1988   88-11821
979.5'00497—dc19   CIP
                                           AC

For their help, the author thanks:

Nellie Broncho, member of the Shoshoni-Bannock tribe

Daisy Dixey, Librarian, Fort Hall (Idaho) Indian Reservation

Karen Jimmy

Ron Mamot, Wind River Rendezvous magazine

Joyce Posey, Secretary of the Shoshoni Business Council, Wind River (Wyoming) Indian Reservation

John Washakie, Chairman, Shoshoni Business Council, Wind River (Wyoming) Indian Reservation

Childrens Press®, Chicago
Copyright ©1988 by Regensteiner Publishing Enterprises, Inc.
All rights reserved. Published simultaneously in Canada.
Printed in the United States of America.
1 2 3 4 5 6 7 8 9 10 R 97 96 95 94 93 92 91 90 89

TABLE OF CONTENTS

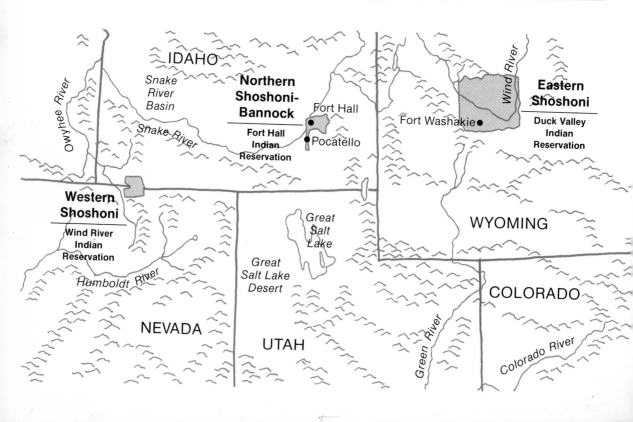

IDAHO

Snake
River
Basin

Snake River

Owyhee River

**Northern
Shoshoni-
Bannock**

**Fort Hall
Indian
Reservation**

Fort Hall

Pocatello

Fort Washakie

Wind River

**Eastern
Shoshoni**

**Duck Valley
Indian
Reservation**

**Western
Shoshoni**

**Wind River
Indian
Reservation**

Humboldt River

Great
Salt
Lake

Great
Salt Lake
Desert

WYOMING

NEVADA

UTAH

Green River

COLORADO

Colorado River

THE SHOSHONI HOMELANDS

The Shoshoni live
mainly in the western
United States. Most
Shoshoni live in Wyoming,
Idaho, and Nevada.

The name *Shoshoni* is
thought to mean "Valley
Dwellers." For thousands
of years, the Shoshoni
roamed the valleys and
mountains of Idaho, Utah,
Nevada, Wyoming, and
Montana.

Alfred Jacob Miller's painting of a Shoshoni preparing a meal

The Shoshoni lived as one with the earth. They took only what they needed from the land.

THE ENDLESS SEARCH FOR FOOD

The Shoshoni for the most part lived in small groups called *bands*. Some bands had only about ten people, all related. Larger bands were made up of several families.

No single place had enough food to support a band. This meant that the Shoshoni could not build

Alfred Jacob Miller's painting of a Shoshoni gathering on the Green River, 1837

permanent villages. They
moved about a great deal
while searching for food.
The Shoshoni obtained
food by hunting and

fishing and by gathering plants. Among the animals they hunted with their bows and arrows were wild sheep, antelope, squirrels, and birds. Some Shoshoni traveled onto the plains and hunted buffalo. Shoshoni fishermen caught salmon and other fish. The Shoshoni also ate roots, seeds, berries, and grasshoppers.

Shoshoni bands were known by the names of their main foods. The members of a band that ate a lot of salmon were called "Salmon Eaters." Those who depended on roots were "Root Eaters." Among the other food names for Shoshoni bands were the "Buffalo Eaters," "Squirrel Eaters," and "Sunflower Seed Eaters."

SHOSHONI HOUSING AND CLOTHING

The Shoshoni lived in a variety of dwellings. Some Shoshoni used branches or animal hides to build their shelters.

Other Shoshoni bands dug shelters out of hillsides.

Modern tepees constructed for a ceremony at Fort Hall, Idaho

Still others lived in tents called tepees, which were made with poles and buffalo skins.

In the summer, the Shoshoni wore little clothing. The men wore only loincloths, while the women wore a kind of apron. In winter the Shoshoni made warm robes out of rabbit and other furs.

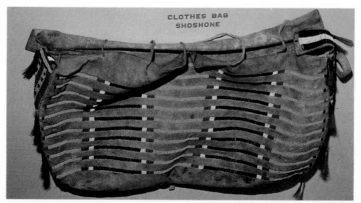

CLOTHES BAG
SHOSHONE

Simple, colorful designs were
beaded on clothing that was worn
on special occasions.

13

SHOSHONI FAMILY LIFE

Many Shoshoni who married went to live with the man's family. Sometimes Shoshoni men and women were allowed to have more than one marriage partner at a time.

Women tanning a hide

Shoshoni women and men had equally important roles in helping the family survive. The men did the hunting. They also served as the chiefs, or leaders, of the bands.

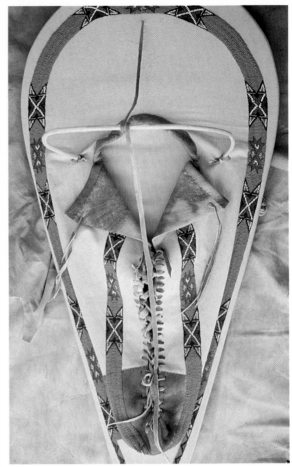

Stella Washakie (left), great-grand-
daughter of Chief Washakie, shows
how a woman carried her baby
on her back in a cradle board.
A modern cradle board (above)

The women did most of
the child raising. They also
did most of the plant

gathering. The Shoshoni used the plants to prepare medicines as well as foods. Medicines made from plants were used to treat everything from heart trouble to ulcers.

Like other Indians, the Shoshoni did not spank or punish their children. They thought that punishment would break the young people's spirits. Shoshoni children rarely misbehaved anyway. They helped their parents with food gathering

and preparation, and with the family's other work.

The Shoshoni had no written language and no schools. Children learned by working alongside adults and by listening to the songs and stories of the elders.

SHOSHONI BELIEFS

The Shoshoni believed in one being called Duma Appáh. This being was also called Our Father or the Creator.

Each morning many Shoshoni faced the Sun in the east and sang a prayer song to Appáh. They believed that the rays of the Sun carried their words up to Appáh.

19

Appáh was said to have created the Earth with the help of the animal nation. Coyote was thought to have created human beings at the time when he had taken on a human form. The Shoshoni believed that, after they died, they went to live in the spirit world.

Tales about the spirit world and the animal nation were told. These stories often had a moral lesson.

The Shoshoni often smoked a sacred pipe when they prayed.

One of the Shoshoni tales talks about the *Nunumbi*, or "Little People." They were thought to kill animals with sticks and stones, and to shoot invisible arrows into people they disliked.

A Shoshoni dancer in traditional dress (left)
A buffalo rib dance stick (above)

RECREATION

The Shoshoni loved to sing, dance, and tell stories. White settlers who came to Shoshoni lands in the 1800s observed them singing as they were fishing. Many of their songs, dances, and stories had religious meaning to the Shoshoni.

The Shoshoni also loved games and sports. The "hand game" was very popular. A small object was passed from player to player. The guesser had to figure out who was holding it and who was pretending. The Shoshoni also played a kind of football with a ball made of animal skin stuffed with

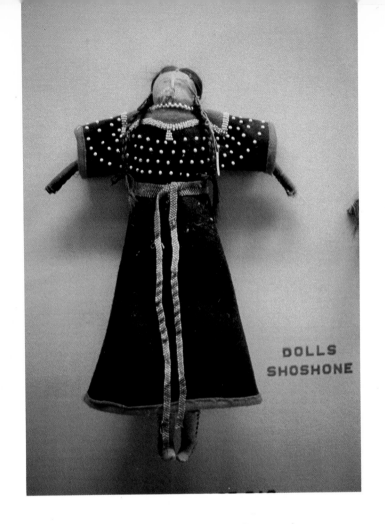

DOLLS
SHOSHONE

rabbit hair. Shoshoni
children liked to run races,
juggle mud balls, and
throw their fathers' arrows
at targets.

THE SHOSHONI
CAPTURE HORSES

During the 1500s Spanish
explorers brought horses
to America. The horses
bred, and soon were roaming
through what is now the
western United States. Some
Shoshoni began capturing
horses about 1600.

Horses still have an important place in Shoshoni life. At special times they are dressed almost as well as their riders.

About 1700 one group of Shoshoni that had horses moved southward. These Shoshoni became a separate tribe—the Comanches. But most Shoshoni remained in the northwest.

THE WHITE PEOPLE ARRIVE

The Shoshoni had little
to do with white people
until the early 1800s. In
1804 President Thomas
Jefferson sent two men to
explore what is now the
northwestern United States.
The two were Meriwether
Lewis and William Clark.
They set out from Missouri
in spring of 1804 and
headed northwest.

In North Dakota Lewis

and Clark asked a teenaged Shoshoni woman named Sacagawea to join them. Sacagawea had been kidnapped from the Shoshoni during a raid in about 1800. She had lived with other Indians since then, as well as with a French fur trader she had been forced to marry. Lewis and Clark wanted Sacagawea to guide them through Shoshoni lands and to act as an interpreter.

An artist's idea of
how Sacagawea might
have looked around 1805.

Sacagawea was a great
help to the Lewis and
Clark Expedition. She dug
up roots and found berries
to help feed Lewis and
Clark and their men. Once
when a boat tipped in the
Missouri River she saved

29

the supplies from floating off. But Sacagawea performed her greatest service for Lewis and Clark in 1805.

In August the expedition met a large force of Shoshoni warriors near the border of Montana and Idaho. Some of the Indians reached for their bows, ready to attack. This was an important moment in U.S. history. If the American expedition had

C.M. Russell's painting of Lewis and Clark meeting Indians in Montana (Lewis and Clark are at extreme right of picture).

been wiped out, England might have tried to claim what became the northwestern United States.

Sacagawea yelled out happily when she saw the

Indians, because they were her people. The chief was her brother, Cameahwait. Instead of attacking, the Indians sold Lewis and Clark the horses needed to reach the Pacific Ocean.

Sacagawea had helped make the Lewis and Clark Expedition a success. But this exploration eventually opened the way for American settlers to seize Shoshoni lands.

THE SHOSHONI ARE PUSHED OFF THEIR LANDS

The American Northwest became part of the United States. Only a few white people came to Shoshoni lands in the early 1800s.

Shoshoni encampment in the southern foothills of the Wind River Mountains in Wyoming

First came people who
wanted valuable furs from
beavers and other animals.
Some of these people
trapped the animals
themselves. Others traded
beads, fishhooks, and tools
to the Shoshoni in
exchange for the furs.

The white fur traders
and trappers got along
well with the Shoshoni. A
few of them married
Shoshoni women. But
during the mid-1800s more

White traders were the first to bring beads to the Indians, who used them to decorate their clothing.

and more white people entered Shoshoni lands. Some whites went there to farm or mine. Others passed over the Oregon Trail that led to California and Oregon. By the 1850s

Pioneers going west along the Oregon Trail

several wagon trails cut through Shoshoni lands.

At first, the Shoshoni were friendly toward the whites. But a number of the white people were cruel to the Indians. Some who hated Indians fired upon the Shoshoni for no reason. Others shot and

Buffalo hide painting of the Sun Dance painted by George Washakie about 1900. The Shoshoni performed the Sun Dance every year to bring the buffalo back to their lands.

ate the animals that the Shoshoni needed for food.

In turn, Chief Pocatello and some other Shoshoni tried to drive the non-Indians off Indian lands. But most Shoshoni followed the

Washakie, chief of
the Eastern Band of
the Wyoming Shoshoni

advice of Chief Washakie
(1804?-1900). Although
he was a great warrior,
Washakie knew that his
people could not drive out
the American soldiers who
patrolled Shoshoni lands.

C.C. Nahl's painting of the southern Idaho Shoshoni signing a treaty in 1866

Washakie told his people to avoid fights with the American settlers and soldiers.

During the 1860s the Shoshoni signed treaties with the U.S. government. By then, the great herds of buffalo that served as a food source had been destroyed. The Shoshoni sold much of their land in the northwestern United States. In return they received food and supplies that they badly needed. The Shoshoni were placed on several *reservations*.

From the start, reservation life was hard for the Shoshoni. Many died of disease and starvation. The Shoshoni also had trouble finding jobs and earning enough money to support their families.

THE SHOSHONI TODAY

Today, there are about 10,000 Shoshoni Indians. Several thousand live on two reservations. One is the Wind River Indian Reservation in Wyoming.

The other is the Fort Hall Indian Reservation in Idaho, which the Shoshoni share with the Bannock tribe. Shoshoni also live on the Duck Valley Indian Reservation at the border of Idaho and Nevada. Thousands more are scattered across the United States.

The map of the United States contains many place names handed down from the Shoshoni Indians.

The towns of Pocatello (Idaho) and Fort Washakie (Wyoming) are named for Shoshoni chiefs. Wyoming has a town called Shoshoni and a woodland area called the Shoshoni National Forest. The

The Shoshoni are proud of their heritage. Each year many return to the reservations to celebrate their traditions and honor those who have brought pride to the tribe. Their accomplishments rank just as high as those of Sacagawea (bottom right) and Chief Washakie.

Shoshoni Falls in Idaho and the Shoshone River and Shoshone Lake in Wyoming are three other landmarks that were named for the Shoshoni Indians.

Mountain peaks in Montana, Wyoming, Oregon, and Idaho are named for Sacagawea. A lake in North Dakota is also named for the young Shoshoni woman who played an important role in American history.

WORDS YOU SHOULD KNOW

Appáh(AP • ee) — the main being of the Shoshoni, also called Our Father or the Creator

Bannocks(BAN • ucks) — a tribe that shares the Fort Hall Indian Reservation in Idaho with the Shoshoni

chiefs(CHEEFS) — leaders

Comanches(kuh • MAN • chees) — a people who broke off from the Shoshoni in about 1700 and moved south to Texas where they became a separate tribe

Coyote(kye • YOH • tee) — a creature who was believed to have created people

fur traders(FER TRAY • derz) — people who came to trade with the Indians for furs

fur trappers(FER TRAP • perz) — people who came to kill fur-bearing animals

Nunumbi(nuh • NUM • bee) — the "Little People," who were troublesome beings

reservations(rez • er • VAY • shunz) — areas set aside by the government for Indians

Sacagawea(sack • uh • jah • WEE • ah) — a young Indian woman who helped the Lewis and Clark Expedition

Shoshoni(show • SHOW • nee) — an Indian tribe that lives mainly in the western United States

Snake Indians(SNAYKE IN • dee • enz) — a nickname white settlers gave to Shoshoni along the Snake River

tepees(TEE • peez) — tents

Washakie(WAH • sha • kee) — a great Shoshoni chief who was friendly toward the whites

INDEX

47

About the Author

Dennis Fradin attended Northwestern University on a partial creative scholarship and was graduated in 1967. His previous books include the Young People's Stories of Our States series for Childrens Press, and Bad Luck Tony for Prentice-Hall. In the True book series Dennis has written about astronomy, farming, comets, archaeology, movies, space colonies, the space lab, explorers, and pioneers. He is married and the father of three children.

CHILDRENS PRESS

50495

9 780516 411569

ISBN 0-516-41156-X

A New True Book

THE MOHAWK